50 THINGS BOOK SERIES REVIEWS FROM READERS

I recently downloaded a couple of books from this series to read over the weekend thinking I would read just one or two. However, I so loved the books that I read all the six books I had downloaded in one go and ended up downloading a few more today. Written by different authors, the books offer practical advice on how you can perform or achieve certain goals in life, which in this case is how to have a better life.

The information is simple to digest and learn from, and is incredibly useful. There are also resources listed at the end of the book that you can use to get more information.

50 Things To Know To Have A Better Life: Self-Improvement Made Easy!

Author Dannii Cohen

This book is very helpful and provides simple tips on how to improve your everyday life. I found it to be useful in improving my overall attitude.

50 Things to Know For Your Mindfulness & Meditation Journey
Author Nina Edmondso

Quick read with 50 short and easy tips for what to think about before starting to homeschool.

50 Things to Know About Getting Started with Homeschool by Author Amanda Walton

I really enjoyed the voice of the narrator, she speaks in a soothing tone. The book is a really great reminder of things we might have known we could do during stressful times, but forgot over the years.

Author Harmony Hawaii

There is so much waste in our society today. Everyone should be forced to read this book. I know I am passing it on to my family.

50 Things to Know to Downsize Your Life: How To Downsize, Organize, And Get Back to Basics

Author Lisa Rusczyk Ed. D.

Great book to get you motivated and understand why you may be losing motivation. Great for that person who wants to start getting healthy, or just for you when you need motivation while having an established workout routine.

50 Things To Know To Stick With A Workout: Motivational Tips To Start The New You Today

Author Sarah Hughes

50 Things to Know

50 THINGS TO KNOW ABOUT BEING AN AU PAIR

Discover How Being an Au Pair Can Change Your Life Forever

Natalie Castle

50 Things to Know About Being an Au Pair Copyright © 2021 by CZYK Publishing LLC.
All Rights Reserved.

All rights reserved. No part of this book may be reproduced in any form or by any electronic or mechanical means including information storage and retrieval systems, without permission in writing from the author. The only exception is by a reviewer, who may quote short excerpts in a review.

The statements in this book are of the authors and may not be the views of CZYK Publishing or 50 Things to Know.

Cover designed by: Ivana Stamenkovic
Cover Image: https://pixabay.com/photos/adult-mother-daughter-beach-kids-1807500/

CZYK
PUBLISHING

CZYK Publishing Since 2011.
CZYKPublishing.com
50 Things to Know

Lock Haven, PA
All rights reserved.
ISBN: 9798722305190

50 THINGS TO KNOW ABOUT BEING AN AU PAIR

BOOK DESCRIPTION

Have you always wondered what an au pair is and what they do? Have you thought about being an au pair before? Are you nervous or anxious about moving away to become an au pair? If you answered yes to any of these questions then this book is for you.

50 Things to Know About Being an Au Pair by author Natalie Castle offers an approach to help you through the process of becoming an au pair, as well as offers helpful tips and advice on how to be the best au pair possible.

Most books on being an au pair tell you all the amazing things you will experience, but never give you practical advice. Although there's nothing wrong with that, this book tells you how to become an au pair with wisdom and practical knowledge, along with the author sharing personal experiences with you to show you everything you need to know. Based on knowledge from the world's leading experts, being an au pair is a great way to experience a cultural exchange program and a great opportunity to travel.

In these pages you'll discover what an au pair is and exactly how to get the most out of this once in a lifetime experience. This book will help you through every step of the process of becoming an au pair such as visa help, helping you find a host family, and showing you how to defeat homesickness and cultural shock.

By the time you finish this book, you will know exactly what to expect when working as an au pair. So grab YOUR copy today. You'll be glad you did.

TABLE OF CONTENTS

50 Things to Know
Book Series
Reviews from Readers
BOOK DESCRIPTION
TABLE OF CONTENTS
DEDICATION
ABOUT THE AUTHOR
INTRODUCTION
1. You Will Need To Do Hours of Research
2. Setting Up a Profile On An Au Pair Website Is Crucial
3. Always Make Sure To Use A Reputable Website
4. Always Video Chat With The Family Before Agreeing To Work With Them
5. Sign A Contract
6. Most Countries Will Require A Visa
7. A Trip to Your Local Embassy May be Required
8. You May Need To Drive As An Au Pair
9. You Probably Will Not Be Paid Very Much
10. Childcare Is Your Main Task
11. You Will Not Be Required To Do Domestic Chores
12. Most Families Will Have A Domestic Helper

13. Even Though Cleaning is Not Your Main Job, Always Clean After Yourself
14. You Are Not A Personal Assistant
15. If You Feel Your Contract Is Not Being Followed, Talk To The Family
16. If You Are Having Major Problems, You Can Leave
17. You May Be Required To Take Language Classes
18. No Previous Language Skills Are Required
19. Many Parents Want You To Teach Their Children Your Language
20. Some Families May Not Speak The Same Language As You
21. If Your Family Does Not Speak Your Language, You Will Learn The Local Language Faster
22. Making Friends May Be Hard At The Beginning
23. Paid Vacation Is Part of Your Contract
24. The School Calendar is Different in Every Country
25. You Are Only Required To Work 5-6 Hours A Day
26. You Do Not Have to Work Weekends
27. Not All Au Pairs Live With The Family
28. No Matter Where you Live, You Are Entitled To Your Own Room

29. Being An Au Pair Is A Great Travel Opportunity
30. Some Families Pay For Your Language Classes
31. Some Families Also Pay For Flights
32. Talk To Previous Au Pairs
33. Offer To Give The Families You Talk To References
34. You Will Create Friendships From People All Over the World
35. You May Have New Rules
36. Always Ask Permission
37. Be A Good Example
38. Vacationing With The Family May Be Needed
39. You Are Always Allowed To Have Time To Practice Your Religion
40. You Are Not Required To Attend Religious Services With The Family
41. There Are More Host Families Than Au Pairs
42. Contract Negotiation Is Normal
43. You Will Have To Grow Up
44. Public Transport Is Scary At First
45. You Might Have To Change Your Wardrobe
46. Feeling Awkward is Normal At The Beginning
47. Being Open Minded Is Important
48. You Will Get Homesick
49. Bring Books
50. It Will Be The Best Experience Of Your Life

Other Helpful Resources
50 Things to Know

ABOUT THE AUTHOR

Natalie Castle is an avid traveler and has traveled to over thirty countries including Thailand, Cambodia, Mexico, Belize, Tanzania, South Africa, Italy, Sweden, and many others.

When she was twenty-one years old she packed up her life and moved to France for an entire year to become an au pair. She did not speak any French and had never been to France before. However, her time in France allowed her to grow into an independent woman and taught her how to travel solo. She will forever view her time in France as the year she fundamentally changed as a person.

After leaving France, she came back to The United States where she completed a degree in education. She has sense worked as an English as a Second Language teacher in countries like Thailand and Tanzania. She also helps create content and curriculum for nonprofit schools in developing countries.

She spends her free time hiking, reading, and always planning her next trip. She is passionate about finding ways to provide healthcare and education to those who need it the most. Although she is passionate about teaching English, her major life goal is to begin working in the medical field and one day build a clinic that focuses on children's and women's health care.

She currently spends half of each year at her home in Florida, and the other half of the year working and volunteering in Uganda. She is currently working for an educational nonprofit that wants to build a clinic as well. She hopes to one day be a nurse in the clinic and help provide quality medical care to the people of Uganda.

You can view her travel and au pair photos on Instagram by searching @nataliemoriah.

INTRODUCTION

"Do the best you can until you know better. Then when you know better, do better."

Maya Angelou

Before we get into the fifty things you must know about being an au pair, let me explain a little more about what an au pair is. Depending on your home country, you may know exactly what an au pair does, know someone who has been an au pair, or maybe even had an au pair when you were a child. In The United States, au pairs are few and far between. Although the knowledge of au pairs is growing, it is still not as widely known in America as it is in Europe and Australia. I had never heard of an au pair before and really did not know the opportunities it could give me. I learned about being an au pair through a travel blog that I regularly followed. I knew as soon as I discovered the concept of an au pair- that I had to become one.

An au pair is a young woman or man (usually between the ages of eighteen-thirty) that moves to a different country to work for a local family by providing childcare in exchange for room, board, and food. The destination country you live in will determine how long you can stay, but most au pairs usually stay between three months to two years.

As part of the job description, you will be taking care of children twenty-thirty hours a a week; so enjoying being around children is an essential requirement. However, previous extensive childcare or babysitting experience is not necessary. Host families know that au pairs are coming as part of a cultural exchange program, not to work as a nanny.

Your nationality will determine which countries you can work in as an au pair. Americans are able to work as an au pair in most countries in Europe, Australia, and New Zealand. Au pairs of other nationalities can work in South Africa and Canada as well. Your nationality and destination country will also determine which visa you will apply for and receive. Visas can be au pair visas, student visas, or working holiday visas.

I decided to go to France on my journey as an au pair for a few reasons. I had always wanted to visit France and was extremely interested about learning about the French culture and language. France is one of the most popular countries where au pairs work, so I knew there were would be a large amount of host families to choose from. Au pairs live all over France, so the concept is largely well known and respected among the French people.

The country and the family that you choose will be the two most important decisions you will make in regards to being an au pair. Explore many countries before choosing one. Once you choose the country, talk to many families from many different cities. Families live in large cities, small towns, rural areas, and villages. There is every environment possible. Each has unique opportunities.

This book was written in the hopes that it will encourage young people to go out into the world and experience life around them. There are many opportunities to travel and experience different countries and cultures. Unfortunately, many young people do not know how to take advantage of these opportunities or are anxious to leave their homes. Traveling when you are young can give you a unique perspective as you learn about people and their way of life.

One of the main determents to young people when deciding not to travel is because they feel the need to complete college as soon as possible and enter the work field. Graduating from college is an amazing goal to have and necessary to land a well paying job in today's society. However, many successful people take a gap year before or during college in order to travel and see the world. Most people have expressed that if they did not travel during college, they probably would not have travelled at all. This poses the popular question: "If not now, when?"

Traveling before college may also give young people necessary means to help them learn what they want to study and which degree they want to earn. Many people who study abroad or take a gap year end up changing their college major after returning home.

When a young person travels, they also gain experiences and knowledge that are hard to learn within the four walls of a classroom. Traveling expands the horizons of learning about religion, language, culture, and race.

Traveling can allow young people to be more successful than their fellow students who do not. This is because people who travel often can usually embrace change better. They can also thrive outside of their comfort zones and learn how to work with people from different cultures and countries.

Before working as an au pair, many young men and women only know how to live with their own families or people who are similar to them. As an au pair, a person learns how to be accepting of people who are different from them. They also learn vital life skills such as cooking, caring for children, driving, and being independent.

Being in a new country means you will often experience loneliness or homesickness. This book will teach you how to push through it and use it to your advantage. Remember when these feelings come along, don't give up. They are a normal part of the au pair experience.

From the beginning of the au pair process, all the choices are yours. You get to pick the destination country, the city, and the host family you will be living with. Where have you always wanted to live? What language have you always wanted to learn? Where can you see yourself living and working for the next three months to a year? These are crucial questions to ask yourself.

The steps to becoming an au pair often seem overwhelming and endless, but the practicals steps outlined in this book will make the process easy. However, do not rush through the steps. Make sure you put thought and wisdom into all your decisions.

This is an opportunity of a lifetime and you want to make sure it is everything you want it to be.

    I know too many au pairs who have chosen their host family too quickly, or without talking to them enough. I have met other au pairs who become unhappy in their situation and are too afraid to speak out. Both of these situations are avoidable if you follow the tips in this book.

    You will undoubtedly learn many crucial things about life and the world when you are an au pair. My time in France taught me how to live a fulfilling life with less stress and less worries. In France life is much slower than in my home country of The United States. The people work slower and acknowledge that they work to live, not live to work. They enjoy rich food shared with good friends. They drink expensive wine and make every meal count. They spend their free time with their families, practicing old hobbies and learning new ones.

    In America when we meet someone we often ask "What do you do for work?". We consider someone's job as the ultimate factor of success. A good job brings along good money, attracts a good spouse, and ultimately allows someone to live a good life. This is what I always thought before my time in France anyway.

My friend from England has often said when they meet someone new they ask "Where did you study?". In England, where a person went to university is the mark of their success. It will determine what knowledge they have, what kind of job they will obtain, and what city they will settle down in.

In France people would simply ask "Vous-êtes content?". "Are you happy?". Of course the French people are also curious about the jobs people have and the degrees they hold. Even if they ask these questions, it is always followed by "Vous-êtes content?". "Are you content with your life?".

I cannot remember the last time I asked someone if they were happy, or the last time someone asked me if I was happy. Hearing someone ask me this in France resonated with me deeply. Had I really ever sat down and asked myself if I was happy? I started asking myself this the whole year I was in France. Most of the time the answer was yes. When the answer was no, I decided what could be done to change it immediately.

As you read this book I hope it encourages you and inspires you to take on a new challenge and to step out of your comfort zone. More than that though, I hope this book makes you question whether you are happy or not. I hope it makes you question whether those are around you are happy or not.

Ultimately you are given one life and it should be lived to the fullest. Travel and laugh often. Surround yourself with those who make you feel hopeful and worthy. Learn what makes you happy and go after it.

1. YOU WILL NEED TO DO HOURS OF RESEARCH

Becoming an au pair will require many hours of scouring the internet. This is because there are hundreds of options available of where and when you can start your au pair journey. Most of your time researching will be deciding which country you want to work in as an au pair. Next, you will need to take time finding a host family to live with. This is especially important because the family can make your experience very easy, or very hard. If you have already done some research on becoming an au pair, you probably came across numerous blogs of bad experiences or people telling you how awful their times was. Let me tell you though, for every bad experience, there are ten good ones. Most au pairs have an amazing time with their host family and do not want to leave when the time comes. Keep searching until you find the perfect family for you.

2. SETTING UP A PROFILE ON AN AU PAIR WEBSITE IS CRUCIAL

There are many websites out there that help link au pairs to loving families. Make a profile with many pictures and a good biography that show your personality and uniqueness. Profiles without any photos are much less likely to get viewed. Keep this in mind when looking through host family's profiles too. Choose profiles that have numerous photos of the parents and the children. Write about your personality type, your hobbies, and your likes and dislikes. This will allow a family to know what they have in common with you. After setting up your profile, you can then start browsing families by location, family size, and kid's ages. Some host families only have one child, while some have up to six children. Choose a family size that you are comfortable with and that you think you can handle.

3. ALWAYS MAKE SURE TO USE A REPUTABLE WEBSITE

Most au pair websites are free for the au pair, but some agency websites will charge a minimal fee. If there is a website that is high cost, it is probably a scam. Many websites will charge the host family a fee to search for an au pair though. This is great because it allows au pairs to view families who are serious and ready for an au pair. Always stay safe when using these websites. I have referenced some great ones at the end of this book. If a website asks for personal or sensitive information such as your social security number or your banking information, do not set up an account. Leave the website and try another one.

4. ALWAYS VIDEO CHAT WITH THE FAMILY BEFORE AGREEING TO WORK WITH THEM

After matching with a family and deciding you want to get to know them more, ask to video chat and see them. I video chatted with about ten families before I finally decided on one. It is always a good idea to see their faces and hear how they speak. You should also talk to the children and see how their temperament and behavior aligns with your own. Ask them to give you a tour of their house so you can see where you will be living. If a family is ready for an au pair, they may already have your bedroom furnished and ready. Ask them to show you where you will be sleeping and bathing. Make sure you know which city or suburb they live in and research it. I spent hours on the computer researching after video chatting with each family. I wanted to know exactly where I was going to be living and what opportunities I would have.

5. SIGN A CONTRACT

Always sign a contract with the family so you know exactly what is expected of you. Make sure the contract has your pay, your days off, your paid and unpaid vacation times; as well as the duties you are required to do. Have the parents sign the contract. Most au pair websites will have a contract template for you to use. When you apply for your visa, the contract will often need to be submitted and approved as part of the paperwork.

6. MOST COUNTRIES WILL REQUIRE A VISA

The destination country will decide which type of visa is required. Some countries have au pair visas, while other countries hire au pairs under student visas or working holiday visas. Both types are legit and normal. Your host family should know which visa you need and will help you with the paperwork. The host family should always be willing to help you with visa support if you need it. If they have had an au pair before, then they will have gone through the process and be able to walk you through it. If not, most au pair websites offer a step by step guide on how to obtain the visa and all the paperwork you may need.

7. A TRIP TO YOUR LOCAL EMBASSY MAY BE REQUIRED

Most countries will require you to apply for your visa in person at the nearest embassy to your home. Sometimes this can be in a different state, so make sure you have time and money to travel for this appointment. I am from Florida and the only French embassy in the south part of The United States is in Miami. My appointment was early in the morning, so I went the night before and got a hotel room. Always schedule your visa appointment online in advance. Show up on time and dress professionally as it is basically an interview. Bring all paperwork with you and copies of each paper to keep for yourself. The paperwork requirements will vary by country; but I had to bring passport size photos, my au pair contract, proof of French Language classes to be taken in France, and a bank statement. Depending on your nationality, you may also need to bring a health form signed by your doctor.

8. YOU MAY NEED TO DRIVE AS AN AU PAIR

Many countries in Europe and cities in Australia have public transportation, but some families may give you a car. They may also require you to drive their children. Always ask when talking to the family if driving will be required and make sure you are comfortable with this. European countries allow you to drive with an American license for a year. You may need to have an official translation of your license or an international license to drive in other countries. Ask your host family to check local requirements for you. Also make sure to ask whether the car you will be driving is automatic or manual. While most people in America drive automatic, almost every person in France takes their driving test in a manual car. This means you may need to learn how to drive manual before leaving your home country.

9. YOU PROBABLY WILL NOT BE PAID VERY MUCH

Most families pay their au pair around $80-$150 dollars a week. People coming to America as an au pair get paid more. However, all your living expenses are paid for, so you will not be paying any bills. The host family provides housing, food, gas for the car if you are driving the children, and basic toiletry items. Despite all the bills being paid for, you also won't be able to save much money. Make sure you are financially stable and have some savings before leaving your home country. While most of the money I made was used for traveling during my vacation weeks, I also had to use some of my savings that I earned in America. Remember to keep enough saved to purchase your ticket back home as well.

10. CHILDCARE IS YOUR MAIN TASK

Your main duties while abroad will be caring for the children. Depending on the age of the kids, you might be required to bath them, feed them, help them with homework, clean up after them, and take them to and from school. Always choose a family with ages of children you are comfortable caring for. I cared for two older children, so I never had to bathe them or physically feed them. I cooked basic meals when the parents were away on business, made sure they completed all their homework, made sure they had showered and insisted they went to bed on time. Of course younger children will be more work, but some au pairs prefer young children to teenagers. It is all a personal preference.

11. YOU WILL NOT BE REQUIRED TO DO DOMESTIC CHORES

Remember that you are an au pair, not a maid. You are only required to help with cleaning involving yourself and the children. You should not have to clean the whole house, do the parent's laundry, clean the parent's car, etc. If the family is having a family cleaning day or spring cleaning day, you may be expected to help. You will also be in charge of cleaning your personal spaces, doing your own laundry, and ironing your own clothes.

12. MOST FAMILIES WILL HAVE A DOMESTIC HELPER

Most European and Australian households have someone that cleans, does laundry, and irons a few times a week. This means cleaning and other duties will not fall on your shoulders. Of course it is always nice to ask how you can be helpful around the house. The family I worked for had a woman who came for two hours everyday. She did all the deep cleaning, the laundry, most of the ironing, and changed the sheets. I always cleaned my own room and made sure it was tidy at all times. This is one easy way you can show respect for the family and their home. Remember that the domestic helper should not have to pick up children's toys, wash children's dishes, or need to move many things before vacuuming. They are in charge of the deep general cleaning, not cleaning after the kids.

13. EVEN THOUGH CLEANING IS NOT YOUR MAIN JOB, ALWAYS CLEAN AFTER YOURSELF

Always keep your own bedroom and bathroom tidy. If they let you use a car, always make sure it is washed after you are done with it. Clean your own dishes and be a respectful household member. Cleaning after the kids is also one of your main duties, especially if they are young. Since my children were older, I always had them put their own dishes in the dishwasher and wipe the table after dinner. I always washed the larger dishes like the pots and pans. Younger children may need their laundry done more often or may make bigger messes. Always make sure the children's rooms are clean. If they are young, clean it for them or ask them to help. If they are older children, ask them to clean their own rooms and then check them when they are done.

14. YOU ARE NOT A PERSONAL ASSISTANT

I have heard of some families trying to use their au pair to run errands for them and have them do other things not required of them per their contract. You are not in charge of taking clothes to the dry cleaner, going grocery shopping, or cooking every meal. Always be helpful, but do let anyone take advantage of you. It is completely normal though to go to the grocery store with the mom and help her do the weekly shopping. It is also normal to help the family cook or to have to cook on your own a few times if the parents are out of town. However, everything should be done as a group and as a family, not you alone. If it is your night to cook or you need to cook while the parents out of town, ask them what they would like the children to eat or ask them to make a meal plan to help you know what to cook or prepare. Cooking is not my expertise, so I always requested the parents to make a plan for me of what I should cook.

15. IF YOU FEEL YOUR CONTRACT IS NOT BEING FOLLOWED, TALK TO THE FAMILY

As soon as you notice something in your contract not being respected, immediately bring it up to the parents. Have an open and frank discussion with the contract in hand. Be polite and clear. Many miscommunications can be caused by a language barrier or a cultural difference. These can be easily fixed when you talk through the problem early on. If you allow the contract to be continuously overlooked, it will cause more problems later on. The more you allow the problem to go on, the harder it will be to talk about and fix it. So, always address problems as soon as they are noticed. The family may also have an issue with something that you do. If they bring up an issue with you, talk through how you can fix it. Try not to get too defensive or be upset.

16. IF YOU ARE HAVING MAJOR PROBLEMS, YOU CAN LEAVE

Most large cities have an au pair agency in them. If you have already tried to talk to the family and did not have a good response, go to your local agency and ask for help. You can also go to the local embassy of your home country and explain to them the situation. They can help place you with a new family. One girl in my town was having an awful time with her family and she quickly reported it to a local agency. They quickly helped her find a new family. Some local agencies may charge a small fee for this, this is completely normal. Do not allow the family to disrespect you and do not let them get away with not following the contract. Remember, your contract was submitted when you applied for the visa, so the local government and embassy will have a copy that they can inspect and bring up to the family.

17. YOU MAY BE REQUIRED TO TAKE LANGUAGE CLASSES

If you travel to a country where English is not the primary language, you will probably be required to take language classes as part of your visa agreement. These can be taken at community centers, universities, or with private language tutors. In France, every au pair is given a student visa. This just means you have to take at least six hours of French language classes a week. I know many au pairs who dropped out of their language classes, but I would not recommend this. If you decide to stay longer or apply for another visa to the same country later in life; they may check to see if you followed the requirements for your first visa. I recommend to always follow the requirements for the visa to avoid trouble. If you are not interested in learning a new language, I recommend becoming an au pair in Australia, New Zealand, or The United Kingdom. These countries do not make au pairs participate in language classes, as long as they already have a strong command of English.

18. NO PREVIOUS LANGUAGE SKILLS ARE REQUIRED

Countries do not require that au pairs have previous language skills before going to the country. You can always start with beginner classes and work your way up. Some countries (like Germany) make you take a language test after three months to show that you are progressing. Do not get stressed though, the test done at three months is basic conversational skills only. If you have already been in the country for three months, passing the test should be easy. France did not require me to show that I was adequately learning French. Italy and Spain do not require this three month test either.

19. MANY PARENTS WANT YOU TO TEACH THEIR CHILDREN YOUR LANGUAGE

Many families hire au pairs because they want their child to learn a second language, usually English. Most parents do not want you to formally teach or have lesson plans; they just want you to talk to the children in English and help them with English homework. The host family I worked for really wanted their children to learn English. The older boy already had a solid grasp of English, so most of the lessons I did with him were conversational. I tried to converse with him about topics that I knew he would enjoy such as video games, vacations, and soccer. The younger girl was new to English, so I used a more organized approach. We used workbooks, flashcards, art projects, and board games to gain language skills. After being at school all day and doing homework, the last thing kids want to do is have one more lesson. Try to make it seem more like playing or just do an activity while you are speaking English.

20. SOME FAMILIES MAY NOT SPEAK THE SAME LANGUAGE AS YOU

Many residents of Europe and Canada are bilingual, but sometimes there are families who only speak their primary language. This can make your move more difficult, but not impossible. When you video chat, you should be able to see the families language skills and decide what you are comfortable with. Both of the parents in my host family spoke exceptional English. This made it easier for me to talk to them and see what they were like as people.

21. IF YOUR FAMILY DOES NOT SPEAK YOUR LANGUAGE, YOU WILL LEARN THE LOCAL LANGUAGE FASTER

Oftentimes au pairs pick a family because the family speaks English and it makes living with them easier. Remember though, this may hinder you from learning the new language because you can speak English with the family. Most host families want to practice their English skills, which means they will eagerly only speak English with you. Even if the parents speak English, make it clear that you would like to practice the local language with them so you can learn it quicker. If you are required to speak English with the children and then also only speaking English with the parents, you may not really end up learning a second language at all.

22. MAKING FRIENDS MAY BE HARD AT THE BEGINNING

You may get lonely the first few weeks you are there, this is normal. Join local Expat groups and go to language classes so you can meet friends quickly and easily. I made most of my friends from my language classes that I took at the local university and community center. I also joined a resource center where I took art classes. This allowed me to meet French friends and helped me to know the local community better. Expat groups can be found online. They are centered towards helping foreign people in new countries make friends. These groups will usually have designated meet up times or excursions that they do each week. I was able to make two really good friends on these websites. Try to make friends with local people as well. This will help you practice your new language and allow you to feel more comfortable making conversations.

23. PAID VACATION IS PART OF YOUR CONTRACT

Unlike many American jobs, most European au pair jobs will grant you two weeks paid vacation for every six months you work. Make sure this is part of your contract when you sign it. Every country differs on paid vacation rules, but you are entitled to have them. Check with your embassy and destination country. My host family gave me all four weeks at the same time, because they were taking a family vacation during this time. This means I could spend one whole month of my time to travel all around Europe. Some families like to put all the au pair's vacation together and other families like to split it up.

24. THE SCHOOL CALENDAR IS DIFFERENT IN EVERY COUNTRY

In Europe, most schools will have the kids go to school six weeks and then have two weeks vacation. So, every six weeks you will most likely have two weeks with the kids at home and not at school. Try to have many activities and fun things planned to keep them occupied. In The United States and Australia, children will have the summer months off. Remember in Australia, summer is the opposite of America and Canada. So children and au pairs in Australia will have Christmas and summer vacations at the same time.

25. YOU ARE ONLY REQUIRED TO WORK 5-6 HOURS A DAY

Most au pair contracts will stipulate how many hours you are required to work each day, it should not be more than five or six. This includes days when the kids are on holiday and not in school. Children in Europe go to school a few more hours than children in other countries. The children I took care of went to school from about 8:30am-5:00pm. They usually went to bed around 9:00 or 9:30. I would usually work about an hour and a half in the morning and then four hours at night. Despite this rule, make sure to remain flexible. Sometimes the parents may need you more during vacation weeks. In exchange, they will probably give you an extra day off during the following weeks. When you know a change in schedule or a vacation week is coming up, ask them the plans ahead of time.

26. YOU DO NOT HAVE TO WORK WEEKENDS

Saturdays and Sunday are your days off. Remember that you will live in the same home as the family, so you need to make clear guidelines about when you are not at work. This way the children know that you have your alone time on the weekends. Since my children were older, this was never really a problem. However, my friends that lived in homes with young children had to remind the kids often that weekends were for alone time or their time with friends. If the children are constantly bombarding you or coming into your personal space during your off days, politely ask the parents to help you talk to the children about the rules. Parents should always make it clear to the children that even though you are home, you are not to be bothered.

27. NOT ALL AU PAIRS LIVE WITH THE FAMILY

In large cities, some families will rent their au pair a room in a shared apartment with someone close to their age. This gives you more freedom and alone time. However, it can also make it harder for you to feel integrated as part of the family. Always clarify with the family where you will be staying before arriving. I had an au pair friend who lived in an apartment about a fifteen minute walk from her host family. She lived with one other girl who was studying at the local university. She was able to make friends extremely easily because she could go out on weekdays, have get togethers on the weekends, and had a local girl as a roommate. However, she also had to get up earlier to factor in commute time, often did not feel very close to the family, and did not have any personal space in the family home. For example, some nights she was required to stay late at the family home and spend the night once a month. Since she did not have a room in the house, she slept on the couch those nights. She did not mind at all because it happened rarely, but some people would always want to be in their own bed. Make the right decision for yourself.

28. NO MATTER WHERE YOU LIVE, YOU ARE ENTITLED TO YOUR OWN ROOM

Per au pair contract rules, au pairs are required to have their own room. They are not allowed to share a room with a family member or anyone else. You may, however, share a bathroom with the children. Your room should have all the basic furnishings you need. This means a bed, a desk, a place to keep your clothes, and a lamp. You can always bring some decorations and pictures from home to help it feel like your room. Always make sure to ask before nailing anything into the walls. If you need something in your room to feel more comfortable, simply ask the family. The majority of host families are very accommodating and want you to feel at home.

29. BEING AN AU PAIR IS A GREAT TRAVEL OPPORTUNITY

During your paid time off, you will have many opportunities to travel. All au pairs have ample time to travel, but au pairs who live in Europe have the most opportunity. Europe has cheap trains and flights to nearby European countries. Always ask the family when your weeks off are, so you have time to plan. During my time in France; I had time to travel to England, Ireland, Spain, Italy, Belgium, The Netherlands, Norway, and Sweden. Make the most of your vacation time and visit a place you have always wanted to see. If you have extended vacation time and are feeling homesick, you can also use your vacation weeks to go back home and visit for awhile. However, going home may make it harder to return to your work as an au pair.

30. SOME FAMILIES PAY FOR YOUR LANGUAGE CLASSES

Although not required, many families will pay for their au pair's language classes if required for the visa. Other families will offer to pay a portion of them. Always clarify who is paying ahead of time and have it stated in the contract. If your family does not offer to pay, do not worry. Most languages classes, even in big cities, are cheap. The local resource center I took classes at was only $40 per trimester or per three months. University classes will be the most expensive option, potentially 500 euros per semester or more. University classes are usually much more strict and well funded though, so you will often learn quicker in these settings. You can also hire a private tutor or find a few friends and hire a tutor for the group.

31. SOME FAMILIES ALSO PAY FOR FLIGHTS

This is also not required, but some families will offer this. Again, make sure it is written in your contract. Many families will write in their profiles what they are willing and not willing to pay for. The host family paying for flights is getting more and more rare. The last few au pairs I have spoken to paid for their flights themselves. The host family paying for your flight is definitely not a requirement, so do not push any family to do this. It is considered more of a perk.

32. TALK TO PREVIOUS AU PAIRS

If the family has had au pairs before, ask if you can have their email or phone number to talk to them. If you are their first au pair, ask them for references (professional or personal), this way you can discover more about them. I was my family's first au pair so I could not talk to any previous au pairs. Instead, my host mom gave me the number of a foreign exchange student they had hosted. I was also able to talk to an American woman who had hosted my host family's son previously.

33. OFFER TO GIVE THE FAMILIES YOU TALK TO REFERENCES

Just like you want to learn as much as you can about them before moving; they want to know about you too. Offer to give them previous work or education references. Giving them previous childcare references like babysitting is even better. I gave my host family one reference for someone I had babysat for and one for a child I tutored the year before. If you are giving references, always ask the person before you give out their number or email. If the host family does not speak English or speaks limited English, make sure to tell the person you are requesting the reference from. This way they can write the email accordingly or speak slowly when on the phone.

34. YOU WILL CREATE FRIENDSHIPS FROM PEOPLE ALL OVER THE WORLD

Your language classes will be a great opportunity to make friends. Since these people are also learning the new country's language; they will be from all over the world. By the time your au pair journey is over, you will have made friends that live on all corners of the earth. I was able to make friends from Germany, England, Poland, Yemen, Brazil, Colombia, and Nigeria. I keep in touch with many of them and have been able to visit them even years later.

35. YOU MAY HAVE NEW RULES

Your host family will probably live a little different than you, this means they have house rules that are different from your own and from your parent's rules. Make sure to discuss any rules or curfews shortly after arriving or before landing. Some families will be more strict than others. If you feel the rules are too strict or too imposing on your freedoms, sit down with the family and discuss how you feel.

Try to reach a compromise with them. Even if they allow you to go out at night, never come home intoxicated and never drive their car if you feel you had too much to drink. Simply let them know you are planning on spending the night out and will be home the next day.

36. ALWAYS ASK PERMISSION

If you want to have a friend over, borrow the car, or go out at night, always ask for permission. The majority of host families will acknowledge that you are an adult and will probably not impose strict rules or curfews. However, it is always a good idea to ask for permission before leaving or inviting someone to spend the night. My host family did not impose a curfew for me, but always asked that I text or call if I would not be returning home or if I would be returning home very late. They also asked that I not have friends over when they were out of town. They were super flexible and actually more relaxed than my own parents, so I had more freedom than I did living in America.

37. BE A GOOD EXAMPLE

Host families will hire au pairs based off morals and values. You will be spending many hours alone with their children and they want to make sure you will be a good example and enforce their family rules. Never curse, dress inappropriate, or be crude in front of the children. If you want to watch a movie or television show that is not age appropriate for the children, watch it in your room and use headphones. Most European families are relaxed about drinking, but always discuss when and where it is okay for you to drink, especially when the children are around. My host family let me drink at dinner when they were drinking and on weekends when I was off duty. Never drink if you are alone with the children or if you will be driving the children.

38. VACATIONING WITH THE FAMILY MAY BE NEEDED

Most families will take a vacation during the time you are with them. Some families like to vacation alone, while others will want to bring the au pair with them. Remember even on vacation, you are only required to work five to six hours a day and are entitled to weekends (or two days off) a week. If both or one of your host parents works weekends, they will give you another two days off during the week. Vacationing with the family is a great way to see other parts of the country and meet their extended family members. It will make you feel more like a family member, so always go with them if they invite you. Sometimes the family will invite the au pair with them and make it clear that they are not required to have childcare duties since the parents will be there. Other times the parents will invite you and expect you to perform you duties with the children.

39. YOU ARE ALWAYS ALLOWED TO HAVE TIME TO PRACTICE YOUR RELIGION

If you need certain days off or want to attend a religious service during the week, tell the family. Most host families are very accommodating as long as they know ahead of time. If you want to get involved with a church or local organization, the family will also help you know where to go. There was an English speaking church in the town that I lived, so I went some Sundays. My host family was always very respectful of my beliefs and let me go to church whenever I wanted.

40. YOU ARE NOT REQUIRED TO ATTEND RELIGIOUS SERVICES WITH THE FAMILY

If your host family is a different religion than you and you do not want to attend services with them, politely explain that you are uncomfortable or do not want to go. You are never required to attend a religious event that is not in agreement with your personal beliefs. This is usually a standard clause in the au pair contract, but always double check that it is there. If you want to attend church or another religious event with the family, ask them if you can come along.

41. THERE ARE MORE HOST FAMILIES THAN AU PAIRS

Host families have a harder time finding an au pair than the other way around. This means you can be picky and negotiate your contract. Always take your time finding and deciding on a family. Video chat and email with several families before choosing. Make sure you have all the information that you need and leave no question unanswered. Also have the family video chat with your family. My host dad and the children video chatted with my mom before I left. My host family was always willing to talk to my parents and help us with anything we needed. This is one way you can tell early on how your host family will act when you are in need. If you notice that a family is not wanting to video chat with you or unwilling to talk to your family, this could be an early red flag.

42. CONTRACT NEGOTIATION IS NORMAL

Many au pairs will negotiate contract terms like pay or vacation before signing. It is not rude to ask for a little more pay or something else you feel is needed. However, never be too pushy and stay polite when negotiating terms. Make sure the contract version you sign is the final and updated one. Your host family will sign it and take it to the embassy in their country to get it approved and stamped. Then, they will fax it or email it to you. You will then take it with you to your visa appointment and have it stamped in your home country as well.

43. YOU WILL HAVE TO GROW UP

This will probably be one of your first times living in a different country. You will have children's lives in your hands. This means your time as an au pair will mature you and force you to grow up a little faster. This is a good thing. More responsibility always brings maturation. Although I had many years of childcare experience before my au pair adventure, I had never lived with a family I worked with before.

Living with the family is different than just working for someone. I quickly learned how to cook, clean up after the children, push the children to finish school assignments, and make sure they got to every place on time. It can be stressful at times, but remember you are not alone. The parents are always there to help.

44. PUBLIC TRANSPORT IS SCARY AT FIRST

My time as an au pair was the first time I had ever rode a bus or metro. Chances are you will probably get lost the first few times. Always stay patient and ask for directions if you need them. In my experience, people were very willing to help me when I got lost and eager to make sure I got to the correct destination. I always tried to sit extremely close to the map or the screen that showed the map, so that I could follow it throughout the ride. This is extra important if you do not have a good grasp of the local language yet.

45. YOU MIGHT HAVE TO CHANGE YOUR WARDROBE

Not only are you around children, but you are living with a host dad that is not related to you. This means you should always be dressed modest when around the house. Bring appropriate pajamas to wear around the house when you are not alone in your room. Coming from Florida and living alone, I often walked around my apartment in shorts or a large t-shirt. This is definitely not appropriate when working around a teenage boy and a host father. I made sure to bring a set of pajamas and sweatpants that were okay to wear around both of them. I also recommend not to walk around the house in a short robe or bath towel after showering. Remember this when exercising as well. If you want to work out in tight shorts or sports bras- work out in your room with the door closed.

46. FEELING AWKWARD IS NORMAL AT THE BEGINNING

You are in a new country with a family you do not know. Feeling awkward and nervous at the beginning is normal. Remember the host family probably feels even more anxious than you. I still remember the car ride home when they picked me up from the airport. My ears were extremely clogged from the long flight and the young girl was giggling because she had no idea what we were saying in English. It's a sweet memory that I still remember often. Even though the beginning may be awkward and full of small talk, you will quickly settle in and feel at home.

47. BEING OPEN MINDED IS IMPORTANT

Your host family will be different than you in many ways. The culture is also different and may consist of some things that do not make sense to you. Stay open minded and tolerant of these differences. You do not have to agree with everything that they do or think, but remaining open minded will go a long way. When interviewing with the families, make sure you have at least a few things in common. Do they like to stay home or go out on weekends? Do they stay up late or get up early? Are they very active or do they prefer to stay home and watch movies? Of course, you cannot have everything in common; but having a few things in common will help to build a foundation for a relationship that can grow easily.

48. YOU WILL GET HOMESICK

Being away from your country and family will be hard. Feeling homesick is normal and even healthy. If you are missing something from home or feeling down, let your host family know. Allow them to comfort you and help you through your challenges. Before you leave your home country, pack a few things that will help you when you are homesick. This could be a picture of your family, your favorite snack, or anything else that reminds you of home. Your host family will expect you to miss your family sometimes and get emotional, so never be embarrassed about these feelings.

49. BRING BOOKS

Living in a different country means there will not be a huge portion of books in your native language. However, capital cities will usually have multi language bookstores. If Amazon is available in your host country, this is also a good option for ordering books. However, bringing many books from home will at least give you reading material for the first few months.

50. IT WILL BE THE BEST EXPERIENCE OF YOUR LIFE

Becoming an au pair is extremely rewarding. You will get attached to your host family and it will be hard to leave them at the end. However, going back to your home country with a new language, new friends, and new knowledge is invaluable. Remember to take each day as it comes and enjoy every moment. The time will pass fast and you will be wishing you could turn back the clock and relive the experience.

OTHER HELPFUL RESOURCES

Here are some great websites and resources to use to find a host family:

https://www.aupairworld.com/en

https://www.interexchange.org/travel-abroad/au-pair-usa/resources/passport/

https://www.aupaircare.com/stories/aupaircare-resources

Here are some resources to help you travel:

https://www.roadaffair.com/backpacking-europe-itinerary/

https://www.seat61.com/european-train-travel.htm

https://fullsuitcase.com/planning-australia-trip/

Here are some blogs written by awesome au pairs:

https://www.aupairohparis.com/blog/2018/6/28/advice-from-an-third-time-au-pair-by-beth-davies

https://www.carolineinthecityblog.com/2012/05/21/a-day-in-the-life-au-pair/

https://www.travelhackergirl.com/what-you-dont-see-from-au-pairs-facebook-pictures/

Here are some blogs from host families:

http://aupairmom.com

https://culturalcare.com/blog/

https://www.myaupairandme.com/blog/

Helpful resources to make friends in the expat community:

https://www.expat.com

https://www.internations.org

https://goexpat.com

READ OTHER 50 THINGS TO KNOW BOOKS

50 Things to Know About Coping With Stress: By A Mental Health Specialist by Kimberly L. Brownridge

50 Things to Know About Being a Zookeeper: Life of a Zookeeper by Stephanie Fowlie

50 Things to Know About Becoming a Doctor: The Journey from Medical School of the Medical Profession by Tong Liu MD

50 Things to Know About Knitting: Knit, Purl, Tricks & Shortcuts by Christina Fanelli

50 Things to Know

Stay up to date with new releases on Amazon:

https://amzn.to/2VPNGr7

CZYKPublishing.com

50 Things to Know

We'd love to hear what you think about our content! Please leave your honest review of this book on Amazon and Goodreads. We appreciate your positive and constructive feedback. Thank you.